THIS JOURNAL BELONGS TO:

Made in the USA
Columbia, SC
11 December 2019

84701219R10061